Journey to Transformation

Noel Cromhout

Copyright: Noel Cromhout
All Rights Reserved

Scripture taken from New King James Version.
Copyright (C) 1982 by Thomas Nelson, Inc.
Used by permission.
All rights reserved.

ISBN-13: 978-1503045408
ISBN-10: 1503045404

CONTENTS

Foreword

What's it all about?

Chapter 1 : Get Going
Your Journey to Transformation

Chapter 2 : Keep Going
Making Sense of Trials and Temptations

Chapter 3 : Take Time
Help for Daily Devotions

Chapter 4 : Make Connection
Finding Your Place in Christ's Body, the Church

Chapter 5 : Be Filled
Five Benefits the Holy Spirit Brings

Conclusion
Closing thoughts

Foreword

It is true that each of us are shaped by those around us. Also true is the fact that our success in life can usually be attributed to the input we have received from those who have intentionally, lovingly and consistently shaped us. My life is testament to the privilege of having been so shaped by Noel Cromhout.

A true man of God, Noel is the most effective maker of disciples for Christ I have come across in thirty years of ministry life. His profound love for Jesus coupled with a thorough knowledge of the Scriptures has resulted in many followers of Christ, around the globe, learning to know God on a deeper level through the Scriptures. His wise and very practical application of Biblical truth to everyday life is astounding in its effect. Noel is able to plumb the depths of Truth in God's Word and make it accessible, understandable and applicable.

It is with much joy and a rich sense of privilege that I recommend this excellent book to you. I pray you will be impacted by Noel's teachings and words of wisdom as much as I have been.

Lorenzo Agnes
President and CEO I ZOmedia

What's it All About?

The salvation Christ purchased for us on the Cross can be likened to a dramatic rescue operation. The Hero, at great personal price, snatches us from the devil's clutches, forgives our sins, and sets us on our way to heaven!

But, as they say on the TV infomercials, … there's more! God's will for every person who has come to faith in Christ is that we should become conformed to the image of His Son. You see, God is forming a new humanity to display the traits of His beloved Son, Jesus Christ.

A wise person has put it this way:
"God loves us so much,
He accepts us just as we are.
But God loves us too much
to leave us just as we are!"

Once we have been saved, rescued and forgiven, we begin a journey towards Christian maturity, a process of spiritual growth toward Christ-likeness.

The five messages of this book are intended to help us along the way to that goal. May the Lord bless you as you read and apply these principles.

Chapter 1 : Get Going

Your Journey to Transformation

The Bible teaches that God is working towards transformation, both of the world, and of the believer.

The world has to be transformed because sin has wreaked havoc on creation. In Genesis 3:17-19, after Adam and Eve had sinned in the Garden, the Lord said: *"Cursed is the ground for your sake. All your life you will struggle to scratch a living from it. It will grow thorns and thistles for you, though you will eat of its grains."* Such has been the far-reaching, devastating effect of sin.

We read in Romans 8:21: *"Everything on earth was subjected to God's curse. All creation anticipates the day when it will join God's children in glorious freedom from death and decay."* (NLT)

Humanity has to be transformed. Sin brought alienation from God, and death. The Fall affected our very being in relation to our Creator, so that now we are hostile to Him, and we are by nature objects of His wrath. (Ephesians 2:3)

Starting Point

This transformation journey begins at our conversion, when we are born again by the Spirit of God, born to new life through faith in Christ. Paul describes it thus in 2 Corinthians 5:17: *"If any man is in Christ, he is a new creation. The old has gone, the new has come."*

Having come to faith in Christ, we now embark on a journey to become transformed to spiritual maturity, to Christ-likeness.

Someone has well said: "The Lord loves us **so** much, He accepts us just as we are. But, the Lord loves us **too** much to leave us just as we are!"

So let us, as it were, get on the bus, let's get going and travel together as the Lord works these needed changes in us, to make us more like Jesus. Let's do it, because this is God's ultimate purpose for every believer.

Romans 8:29
*"For whom He foreknew, He also predestined to be **conformed to the image of His Son** …"*

Our Model

A great model in this process is the apostle, Peter. When the Lord first met him, He said: *"You are Simon; you shall be called Peter"* (which means rock or stone.) Here we have the hint that the Lord was going to make something solid and strong out of this rough, impetuous-but-likable fisherman.

But the actual process begins a short time later, when the Lord calls Peter and his brother, Andrew, with these words in Mark 1:16-18:
"Follow Me and I will make you become fishers of men."
"Immediately," says Mark, "they left their nets and followed Him."

In other words they "got on the bus" with Jesus.

Not a smooth bus ride

However, it was not going to be a trouble-free journey, this journey to transformation, from Simon, the easily blown-about reed, to Peter the rock! In fact, at one time it looked as though Peter was getting off the bus! On the night before Jesus was crucified, he denied the Lord under pressure three times, remember?

But as we fast-forward to Acts 2, just about six weeks after Christ's crucifixion and resurrection, we read these thrilling words in verse 14: *"But Peter, **taking his stand** with the eleven, lifted up his voice and said, "Fellow Jews and all who live in Jerusalem…"* and he preached on the crucifixion, resurrection and ascension of Jesus.

Notice, this was in the same city, where just 6 weeks previously, Peter caved before a servant and a few soldiers and denied knowing Christ! Now, here he is taking his stand for the Lord, before a crowd of several thousand!

Measurable Change

That same day, we read further, in response to Peter's message, about three thousand people came to faith in Christ and were baptized! Simon the reed had turned into Peter, a rock! Here was measurable change!

Indeed, there was still much to be done regarding Peter's transformation. But the change in him at this stage was marked and he was able to play a truly significant leading role in the early Church, in its rapid expansion of the Gospel.

So, what can we learn from observing Peter's journey to transformation? Before we "get on the bus", we should take note of Jesus' promise to transform us if we surrender to Him: *"You are ….you shall be."* (John 1:42)

Six Features in Peter's Journey

1. Heeding The Call To Get Going on the Transformation Journey.
(Or, in other words, "Getting on the bus!")

Jesus' call to them was: *"Follow Me and I will make you become…"* (Mark 1:16)
Their response? *"At once they **left** their nets…"* (Verse 17)

Getting on the bus with Jesus involves *letting go* of our personal rights and ambitions. In short, it means unconditional surrender to the One Who surrendered Himself to die on the Cross for your sins.

Caution! This doesn't mean you have to leave your job or drop out of college. It *does* mean you relinquish your rights of ownership - He is Lord of your life, and of everything you have and do. *"They left their nets …"*

2. Exposed To Christ's Teaching

Peter and the apostles heard the Lord teach the crowds, and they had Him teach them privately the things concerning the Kingdom of God. We need to be taught the Word of God; we must learn the great doctrines of the Bible. Acts 2:42 *"They continued in the apostles' doctrine ..."*

Transformation involves your own regular reading of the Bible, and ongoing exposure to the teaching of the Word by those gifted by God to do so. Colossians 2:6,7 *"As you therefore have received Christ Jesus the Lord, so walk in Him, rooted and built up in Him and established in the faith, as you have been taught, abounding in it with thanksgiving."*

3. On-The-Job Training

Jesus did not wait for Peter to pass a theological exam. He put him and the other apostles to work early on in their journey, gave them instructions and then had them report back to Him what they had done.

Matthew 10:1 *"He called the twelve to Him and gave them authority to drive out evil spirits and to heal every disease."* Verse 5 tells us: *"These twelve Jesus sent out with the following instructions ..."*

We learn by **listening** to the Word, and we learn by **doing**, serving the Lord. So, get involved in studying and serving in the church and in your neighborhood. That's part of your transformation journey.

4. Receiving Correction

Peter was corrected, along with the other apostles, in regard to seeking for position. When James and John petitioned the Lord for high positions in His Kingdom, Mark records that Peter and the other apostles were angry. Why do you suppose they were so cross with their team mates? I believe it was because they themselves were hoping for the choice positions! The Lord corrected them sternly.

Mark tells us Jesus said, in effect: *"Don't be like the rulers of this world, pushing for position and status … Whoever wants to be great must become a servant … "* (Mark 10: 43-45) Jesus demonstrated this servant attitude at the Last Supper, when He, their Lord, washed His disciples' feet.

Later, Peter was sharply rebuked for wanting to prevent Jesus from going to Jerusalem to be crucified. *"Get behind Me, Satan   ... are an offense to Me! You do not have in n things of God, but the things of men."* (Matthew 16:23)

How would you have reacted to this reprimand? Hopefully, you'd be like Peter. In spite of the embarrassment of this harsh rebuke, he stayed on the bus! He kept following Jesus, and Jesus continued the "making" process in Peter's life.

Getting off, or staying on board? We all need correction from time to time. How we handle it is crucial to our continued growth and transformation.

Proverbs 12:1 says: *"He who hates correction is stupid!"* (NASB) When you're corrected, unpleasant though it may be, remember: it's part of the transformation journey. Stay on the bus! Keep following and He will keep making you.

Abject Failure

All the apostles initially ran away when Jesus was taken by the soldiers and put on trial. But Peter actually cursed and swore that he did not know Jesus when confronted by a servant, and surrounded by a few soldiers. (Mark 14:71) And this, after he had boasted: Matthew 26:35 *"Even if I have to die with you, I will not deny you!"* The fact that Peter then went out and wept bitterly, shows that his denial was due to weakness and inability, it was not willful rejection of his Lord.

A short time later Peter was restored, when Jesus, now risen from the dead, met him on the shore of the lake, and asked him three times: *"Do you love Me?"* Three times, Peter answered, *"Yes, Lord,"* canceling out his three-time public denial of His Master. (John 21:15-17)

5. Back on Board

Peter "left the bus" for a short time. But, sensibly, he boarded the bus again, forgiven, restored, and much wiser. He now had an understanding of his own character weakness, when under pressure. This forced him to rely totally on the Lord, and not to boast of his steadfastness, noble though his intentions were. This was a vital part of his transformation process.

For you and me, the warning from 1st Corinthians 10:12 is very relevant: *"Let him who thinks he stands, take heed, lest he fall."* If you have failed the Lord and "fallen off the bus," get up, run back to the Lord, and apologize. Re-affirm your love for Him, and you will be forgiven and restored, as was the case with Peter.

It Starts Here!

The journey from "Simon" to "Peter" began with Peter's unconditional surrender to Christ. He and Andrew left their nets … and followed Him in obedience to His call. Have you made that total surrender? That's the essential ingredient, the starting point in the transformation of your life.

Peter's journey involved learning God's Word, and getting busy serving the Lord in some way. Is this happening in your life? Do you regularly spend time in the Scriptures? Do you have regular exposure to good Bible teaching? Are you engaged in some sort of ministry?

Being on the bus involves receiving correction when necessary. We must always be open to constructive criticism; it's essential if we are to grow in the Christian life.

If, like Peter, you fail the Lord dismally, don't run from him, instead, run to Him. He is always ready to forgive and restore, if your repentance is genuine. Humbling yourself to confess your sin and repent of it is a vital part of your journey towards being transformed. (1 John 1:9)

6. The Signal Factor

The signal event that marked a measurable change in Peter in his transformation journey was when he was filled with the Holy Spirit. Acts 2:14 records: *"Peter, standing up with the eleven ..."* The same man who just a few weeks before had caved before a servant and a few soldiers and denied knowing Jesus, was now boldly preaching to a very large crowd which had come together in the Temple on hearing the noise of the disciples speaking in other tongues under the Spirit's inspiration.

Jesus had promised His followers: *"You shall receive power after the Holy Spirit comes upon you and you will be My witnesses in Jerusalem, Judea, Samaria and to the uttermost parts of the world."* (Acts 1:8) This was fulfilled in Acts 2:1-4, when Peter, along with the other disciples, was filled with the Holy Ghost. Now, under the Spirit's power, Peter's preaching resulted in 3,000 people turning to Christ and being baptized.

All the other stages in Peter's journey were significant for his progress. But the baptism in the Holy Spirit gave the major impetus to his being changed from unsteady Simon, to firm, solid, rock-like Peter!

The Most Joyous Command In The Bible

"Be filled with the Holy Spirit." (Ephesians 5:18) Someone has said this is the most joyous command in Scripture. Why is this so?

Here are 4 reasons, among many more:

- The Holy Spirit makes Christ more and more real to you. (John 16:14)

- He makes the Scriptures more understandable to you as you read the Bible. (John 16:13)

- It is the Holy Spirit Who makes God's love real to you and through you, to others. (Romans 5:5)

- Above all, He empowers you to serve Christ, and to take your stand boldly for the Savior, as the transformed apostle Peter did, when he was filled. (Acts 2, Acts 4)

Don't neglect this command to *"Be filled."* As the Spirit's infilling gave Peter supernatural boldness to stand up for Jesus and to proclaim the Good News fearlessly, so He will empower and embolden you, as you constantly look to Him for this infilling.

The Work goes on

God is doing a transforming work in the world. He is doing a transforming work in people like you and me. Are you ready to get going on this journey of faith and take the journey to transformation? The Lord will change you from a Simon - the unsteady, the fragile reed - to a Peter, steady and strong like a Rock. Get on the bus, stay on the bus, and He will get you to your God-appointed destination in His time.

Here are two Bible references to encourage and instruct you on your journey to maturity:

Philippians 1:6
"Being confident of this very thing, that He who has begun a good work in you will complete it until the day of Jesus Christ;"

Philippians 2:12-13
"Therefore, my beloved, as you have always obeyed, not as in my presence only, but now much more in my absence, work out your own salvation with fear and trembling; for it is God who works in you both to will and to do for His good pleasure."

Your Checkpoint: How are you doing on your journey to transformation toward Christ-likeness?

Make a check mark next to Yes or No for the following questions, with reference to the Scriptures given:

Read Mark 1:16-17 and answer this: Have you truly surrendered to the call of Jesus and "boarded the bus" on your journey to transformation?

  Yes ___ No ___

Are you involved in regular Bible reading and study, both personal and corporate?

  Yes ___ No ___

Are you serving God in your local church? If so, how?

  Yes

_____

_____

  No ___

Read the following passages and answer: Are you open to being corrected on your spiritual journey? Proverbs 12:3; 1 Peter 5:5-7

      Yes ___   No ___

Have you been filled with the Holy Spirit?
Acts 19:1-6; Ephesians 5:18, Luke 11:5-13

      Yes ___   No ___

Are you living a consistent, Spirit-filled life?
Galatians 5:16, 25

      Yes ___   No ___

If you have answered "No" to any of these questions what will you do to stay on the bus to transformation?

_____

_____

_____

_____

Chapter 2 : Keep Going

Making Sense of Trials and Temptations

James 1:2-4
"My brethren, count it all joy when you fall into various trials, knowing that the testing of your faith produces patience. But let patience have its perfect work, that you may be perfect and complete, lacking nothing."

James 1:12-15
"Blessed is the man who endures temptation; for when he has been approved, he will receive the crown of life which the Lord has promised to those who love Him. Let no one say when he is tempted, "I am tempted by God"; for God cannot be tempted by evil, nor does He Himself tempt anyone. But each one is tempted when he is drawn away by his own desires and enticed. Then, when desire has conceived, it gives birth to sin; and sin, when it is full-grown, brings forth death."

"Why is this happening to me?"
"Why doesn't God make the problem go away?"

You've probably asked these questions, just as I have, when the Christian life gets difficult. James' letter is particularly helpful in this regard because in it, he addresses the issues of trials and temptations and helps us make sense out of them as we keep going on our transformation journey to Christian maturity.

What kind?

Firstly we must distinguish between the trial of faith and the temptation to sin. Verse 2 talks about "the testing of your faith." This refers to tough situations, or problems that require trust in the Lord, in the midst of difficult circumstances. Maybe you've lost your job, perhaps you're short on finances, or you're ailing in health. You pray, you do all the right things, but nothing changes. That's the test of faith. You have to keep trusting the Lord, in spite of the circumstances.

Verse 12, on the other hand, refers to the temptation to sin. It relates to the internal - to your desires. It is speaking about, for example, the temptation to curse, to steal, the temptation to cheat on your spouse, … things like that. So, let's look more closely at this matter of trials and temptations – I know the Lord will help us, as we do so.

Beware the Pity Party

Verse 2 says: *"Count it all joy when you have various trials."* We must avoid the inclination to "throw a Pity Party" when our faith is tested - we'll never cope that way. We must remember that it's not necessarily the trial that is our biggest problem, it's our attitude to the trial.

Wallowing in self-pity will almost guarantee our defeat. Rather, as James writes, *"Count it all joy when you fall into various trials."* Does that mean God wants us to burst out laughing with glee over our troubles? Of course not! The Lord is not encouraging flippant behavior. What it means is this: Consider this trial as an opportunity to grow. Have a positive attitude, because Paul goes on, *"You know that the testing of your faith produces endurance or patience."* Keep on believing, keep on trusting, no matter how tough the situation may be. God wants to build endurance into your life. Don't go by feelings; go by faith.

Find a verse or a passage in the Scripture, speak it out, pray it in, hold on in faith. For example, you could take 1 Corinthians 10:13: *"No temptation has overtaken you but such as is common to man; and God is faithful, who will not allow you to be tempted beyond what you are able, but with the temptation will provide the way of escape also, so that you will be able to endure it."*

Take a hold of that phrase: "God is faithful." Declare it out loud. Thank the Lord that He will see you through. He is utterly dependable and won't allow the weight of the trial to break your back. The verse goes on, *".. but will with the test make a way of escape that you may be able to bear it."*

Develop your muscles

Faith, in my view, is something like a muscle. If we **don't** use our muscles, they atrophy and eventually we **cannot** use them. Through exercise – often strenuous exercise – our muscles develop. We grow strong. But the stress we put on our muscles is not always pleasant. Have you ever watched people working out in the gym? Their faces contort, they sweat, and one almost feels like stepping up and offering to help them ease the strain! Don't do it because they won't thank you! They're developing their muscles, building physical endurance into their bodies. In a similar way, when our faith muscle is tested, we must keep exercising it. As we do so, it grows tougher and stronger and we build up the ability to endure, to persevere, to carry on to the end of the journey.

Your choice

Let me ask you a question: do you want to be a firecracker or a flashlight? Too many professing Christians are like firecrackers: they start off with a bang, but in a short time they just fizzle out. They're eager, they're enthusiastic, they're busy for God for a while, then they drop out, they quit attending meetings. And if you ask them what's wrong, they'll blame someone for hurting or offending them or they'll find some excuse for their failure to carry on. Often, it's that they didn't have a right attitude to the test God allowed to overtake them. Instead of keeping on in faith, they went by their feelings. They looked for someone else to carry them up the mountain, instead of seeing the mountain as an opportunity to exercise their faith muscle and so develop endurance.

In contrast, the flashlight is not at all spectacular. It just gives a steady light in the darkness as it lights your path through the gloom without any noisy display. Don't be like a firecracker that gives a spectacular show and then fizzles out. Rather be like a flashlight - shine steadily for the Lord in your daily life, in all circumstances. Trust Him, not your feelings, and He will keep you shining.

The "Faith" Attitude

"Count it all joy," says the Scripture. Face the trial with a positive attitude. Say something like this: "Lord, I don't like this situation, but I thank You for the opportunity to show that I trust You, not only in good times, but in bad times as well." This is the attitude that pleases the Lord, because our faith honors Him as nothing else can. In fact, the Bible speaks of only two occasions when Jesus "marveled," and in both cases it was related to faith. The first was when the Roman army officer declared his confidence that Jesus could heal his servant just by saying the word, and Jesus then marveled at his faith. The second happened in His hometown of Nazareth. Here we read, *"He could not do many mighty works there. And He marveled because of their unbelief."* In the first case He marveled at the man's faith; in the second, He marveled at the people's lack of faith. Where do you fit in?

Unbelief: how serious!

Think of it this way: When we exercise faith, we are saying, "Lord, I trust You; I believe You are utterly reliable." But unbelief says, "I refuse to depend upon You. I'm not convinced that You are trustworthy!" Have you ever thought of your response in that way? Do you see now why I've said that faith honors the Lord as nothing else can? So, because your faith is so important, the Lord allows it to be tested from time to time, not to destroy us, but to strengthen that ability to trust Him and so to build a "keep on keeping on" ability into our lives.

James continues in verse 4 of chapter 1 to say: *"Let patience [or endurance,] have its perfect work."* The intended goal is that you may be well-rounded as a believer, lacking nothing.

Example, Joseph

Let's have a look at a Bible example of this faith under pressure and see how it worked out for good in the life of one of history's heroes.
Young Joseph, while a teenager, had two visions in which God showed him that his family would one day bow down to him. This came to pass about twenty years later, when Joseph, now Egypt's Prime Minister, second only to Pharaoh, was able to save not only his estranged family, but the whole region from the effects of famine.

Wasted Years?

Twenty-something years - why so long? Were these years wasted? No! God was building something vital into Joseph's character during that time, the faith that would not falter in the severe conditions of drought and famine. Psalm

105 gives us a brief summary of Joseph's calling, of his trials of faith, and of his subsequent success in what God called him to do.

Psalm 105:17-22
"He sent a man before them - Joseph - who was sold as a slave. They hurt his feet with fetters, he was laid in irons. Until the time that his word came to pass, the word of the LORD tested him. The king sent and released him, the ruler of the people let him go free. He made him lord of his house, and ruler of all his possessions, To bind his princes at his pleasure, and teach his elders wisdom."

We cannot cope with weighty responsibilities using baby-sized faith. Our faith must be exercised and strengthened, and endurance must develop, before we can meet those responsibilities.

Joseph faced his trials head on. He kept trusting until the Word came to pass and God then had a mature man of true integrity and courage to act as savior of the land. The trials developed his faith, gave him the ability to persevere and thus fulfill the task God called him to do.

Does that make sense? Can we understand the principle behind the phrase, *"Count it all joy..."*?

Help during the trial

But, you ask, what can I do in order to get through these trials in a God pleasing way? James 1:5 helps us here: *"But if any of you lacks wisdom, let him ask of God, who gives to all generously and without reproach, and it will be given to him."* Isn't that good to know? Ask the Lord and He' will give you the wisdom you need to handle your particular situation properly.

The greatest compliment we can give to our Lord is to trust Him when it's not easy to do so. This will ensure that your faith is not just like a firecracker, starting off with a bang and a bright display, only to fizzle out quickly. Rather, that it glows steady and strong like a flashlight, and that it endures through good times and bad.

Not the Same

Verse 12 is dealing with a different kind of test. This is not a trial of faith in the sense of what we've just talked about. It is concerned with temptation to sin. The former is usually in connection with external circumstances, but this latter test deals with the internal. Let's read verses 13-14: *"Let no one say when he is tempted, "I am tempted by God"; for God cannot be tempted by evil, nor does He Himself tempt anyone. But each one is tempted when he is drawn away by his own desires and enticed."*

Did you notice the words, *"Drawn away by his own desires .."*? Clearly this passage is referring to temptation that appeals to our fallen nature, our flesh, our carnal nature. For example, we're tempted to buy designer clothes we cannot afford; we're tempted to watch movies that arouse our sexual passions; we're tempted to lie to benefit ourselves in some way.

Three Gates

The Bible tells us there are three "gates" or points of access through which the devil tempts us: the eye gate, the appetite gate and the ego gate. Or to put it in Bible language: the lust of the eyes, the lust of the flesh and the pride of life. (1 John 2:15,16)

This is how Eve succumbed to the serpent's temptation in Eden, remember? Genesis 3 states, *"When she saw the tree was good for food and pleasant to the eyes"* - that's the eye gate and the appetite gate - *"and that it was desirable to make one wise"* - the ego gate - *"she took of the forbidden fruit and ate and also gave to her husband and he ate."*

Whose Fault is it?

Now James writes: don't blame God when you're tempted to sin, God is not like that. He'll allow a trial of faith through tough circumstances in order to develop endurance; but He will never tempt you to steal money, lust after someone else's marriage partner or spend a lot of money on something merely to boost your ego. No, the problem is **us**, the carnal nature, our own lusts, our own desires. It's important to understand that.

It's equally important to understand that temptation alone is not necessarily sin. We're tempted when the thought enters our mind. It's like the devil holding up the object of attraction where we can see it, as if looking through the window. But it's still **outside** the house and we can turn away from it, we can draw the curtain and shut him out. But, if we keep looking, if we keep thinking about it, the pull gets stronger and we're drawn away, we're enticed. To continue the metaphor, we actually open the door to the temptation and it takes hold of us. **Then** we're guilty. Sin has been conceived in our hearts and spiritual death is the result.

Prevention is Better Than Cure

Better, far better, to close the curtains before our appetites are aroused. We can do it, and the Word says that we're blessed if we endure the temptation and we will receive the crown of life.

I must reinforce what I said earlier: temptation alone is not sin. We sin when we **entertain** the temptation and then **give in** to it.

Jesus Has Been There, Too!

Our Lord Jesus is proof of this. He was tempted in every way like we are yet He never sinned. It states in Hebrews 4:15: *"For we do not have a high priest who cannot sympathize with our weaknesses, but One who has been tempted in all things as we are, yet without sin."*

Yes, He was tempted: the bait was dangled in front of Him on numerous occasions but He always closed the curtains, He always backed away. Temptation to sin is not sin but don't play with temptation! Back away, right away! Because if you look at the bait for a little while, your carnal desires will take over. You will be pulled towards the sin; the Bible says, *"drawn away and enticed"*. And then, as the saying goes, you're a gonner, you've lost, you've fallen! Then you must not blame God because He doesn't tempt us with evil.

And another thing, don't blame the devil! Don't say, "The devil made me do it!" He may have displayed the bait, but this is the point James is making: our own decisions, our own lusts draw us away and we take the bait, with disastrous results. It's important that we take responsibility for our sins when we give into temptation. 1 John 1:9 assures us: *"If we confess our sins, He is faithful and righteous to forgive us our sins and to cleanse us from all unrighteousness."* But notice: we won't get forgiveness for our excuses, just for our sins!

How?

How then can we deal with temptations that assail us almost daily? Let me share with you how I try to handle it …

Don't trust yourself! You may have been a believer in Jesus for years, you may feel your faith is strong, but 1 Corinthians 10:12 warns us, *"Let him who thinks he stands, take heed lest he fall."* No matter how long we've been following the Lord, our flesh, our carnal nature, doesn't improve. If we grow spiritually careless and give the flesh the smallest opportunity, we can fall.

Learn from David

Remember King David and Bathsheba? David was by this time an older man, but he feasted his eyes on Uriah's wife. He was drawn away by his own lusts and he committed adultery with her. Then he had her husband murdered in an attempt to cover his sin. You see how destructive sin is? Praise God, David later penned Psalm 51, his inspired declaration of true repentance, and God forgave him. But he reaped the consequences of his sin in his old age. Don't be naïve and trust yourself; you could fall too.

What To Do?

When faced with temptation, run! Don't hang around even to pray. Pray as you run! Paul writes to Timothy, *"Flee youthful lusts!"* Whether you're youthful or not, that makes sense, doesn't it? Don't put your hand near the fire and say, "I'm trusting the Lord that I won't get burned!" You will get burned! Get away from the fire! Avoid situations where temptation can capture your thoughts. *"Bring every thought captive to the obedience of Christ."* (2 Corinthians 10:4)

Radical, Man!

If you're tempted by a colleague at work, and you know it's unlawful, change your job.

Wow, you say, that's drastic! Yes it is! Jesus said in Mark 9: *"If your hand causes you to sin, cut it off … It's better for you to enter into life maimed rather than having two hands to go to hell, into the fire that shall never be quenched."* If we're serious about living for Jesus, then we must be serious about avoiding falling into temptation. We want that crown of life, don't we? We don't want to be caught by our sinful desires, so we need to take appropriate steps, however radical, to make sure we don't risk being drawn away and enticed into sin.

Above all

Remember that our sinless Savior, Who is also our High Priest, was tempted in every way that we are, so He understands our struggles. Hebrews 4:15 states, *"For we do not have a High Priest who cannot sympathize with our weaknesses, but was in all points tempted as we are, yet without sin."*

Come then, let us apply verse 16 and we will find His mercy and grace to help us through the trials and keep us going on our transformation journey. Hebrews 4:16 encourages us: *"Let us therefore come boldly to the throne of grace, that we may obtain mercy and find grace to help in time of need."*

Summary

James writes of two kinds of temptation:

The first: where our faith is tested in difficult circumstances. Keep trusting, learn to persevere, to endure, because God is building character.

The second: where the temptation to sin appeals to our carnal nature. Don't blame God. Run away before temptation takes hold and becomes sin. The Lord promises a crown of life to those who endure the trials and temptations of life as we live for Christ in this fallen world.

Your checkpoint: how are you doing on your journey to transformation in Christ-likeness?

How do you react to difficult situations that test your faith?
- Become frustrated?
- Feel sorry for yourself?
- See the trial as an opportunity to grow into Christ-like maturity?

What 3 gates does the devil use to tempt you?

_____

_____

_____

Which of these "gates" give you the most trouble?
- Eye gate?
- Appetite gate?
- Ego gate?

What can you do if you failed to resist the temptation?

_____

_____

_____

What should you do to avoid falling into sin?

_____

_____

_____

Scriptures to help you:

Proverbs 22:3
1 Corinthians 10:13
Psalm 101:3

Chapter 3 : Take Time

Help for Daily Devotions

On our journey to transformation, we need to have a daily diet of Scripture and prayer, i.e., daily devotions, or as some prefer to call it, your regular "quiet time," when you separate yourself to communicate with God.

Consider: God desires that we have a relationship with Him. Jeremiah 31:3 *"… I have loved you with an everlasting love. Therefore with loving kindness I have drawn you."*

The Cross proves that He loves us. Romans 5:8: *"God demonstrates His own love towards us, in that while we were yet sinners, Christ died for us."*

Faith in the Blood that Jesus shed for us gives us access to God's presence. Hebrews 10:19, 22 says, *"…we have boldness to enter the holy place by the Blood of Jesus…"* and *"Let us draw near with a sincere heart in full assurance of faith"*.

So let's do it!

Let's get communicating with the Lord on a regular basis. Here are some suggestions:

CHOOSE a regular time, a regular place.
Daniel prayed 3 times per day, in his roof chamber or upper room. (Daniel 6:10,13) A secluded, undisturbed place where you won't get interrupted, is ideal. The Psalmist prayed in the early morning. Psalm 5:3 *"In the morning, O Lord, You will hear my voice …"*

Early morning is preferable to late at night for those with regular schedules. Better to meet the Lord at the start of the day, before you have to deal with the devil! However, each person must find the time and place that works best for them.

BEGIN with a short prayer of thanks to the Father in Jesus' Name, for His love, His salvation, and for His Word. Ps 100:4 *"Enter His gates with thanksgiving, His courts with praise."*

ASK the Holy Spirit to give you understanding as you read the Bible. John 16:13 *"…He will guide you into all truth."* John 17:17 *"… Your Word is truth."*

READ systematically and consecutively. For example, Ephesians Chapter 1 through to chapter

6, or as far as you can go for that particular session. Next day, pick up where you left off. That way you get everything in proper context, thus ensuring a better understanding of that particular Book, and over time, seeing the bigger picture of God's revelation to us.

MAKE a note of any verse that stands out for you. Later in the day, or week, you can be refreshed by looking it up again. It's something like grabbing a snack-on-the-move between meals, to keep you going.

PRAY these verses back to God; ask Him to work out these truths in your particular situation.

MEMORIZE at least one verse per week. That way, you build a spiritual armory in your life. When you encounter a crisis, the Holy Spirit can bring that word to your mind, you can speak it into the situation and experience God's intervention in the crisis.

PRESENT your needs and petitions to the Lord.
Philippians 4:6 - Your worries.
Philippians 4:13 - Your material and physical needs.
James 1:5 - Your need for wisdom in difficult situations.

PETITION the Lord for your family, your community, for the church where you worship and receive your spiritual provision.

It's important to lift your prayer horizons beyond your own needs, to include the wider concerns of God's people, God's Work, God's Kingdom.

Jesus taught in Matthew 6:9-10
"Pray like this: 'Our Father .. Thy kingdom come .. Thy will be done on earth as it is in heaven."

You can use these words as you pray for others. For example, "Lord, let Your kingdom, Your rule come in my neighbor's life". "Let Your will be done in this Church" or "in this family." Praying as Jesus taught gives both substance and direction to our prayers, and prevents us from becoming locked in to a little world where we see only our own needs.

CLOSE your time of devotions with a **personalized version of a passage** like Psalm 19:14: *"Let the words of my mouth and the meditation of my heart be acceptable in Your sight, oh Lord, my Strength and my Redeemer."*

Another suggestion:
Many believers find the "ACTS" acronym very helpful as a guide in their daily devotions.

- **A** stands for **Adoration**
- **C** stands for **Confession**
- **T** stands for **Thanksgiving**
- **S** stands for **Supplication** (requests, petitions)

Adoration

Begin with a time of worship. Reading out loud portions of a praise psalm, or a passage like Revelation 5:9-14, and making these words your own, can be very helpful.

Confession

If you're aware of having sinned in any way, whether in attitude or in actions, don't make excuses. Tell the Lord you're sorry, and thank Him for His forgiveness: 1 John 1:9 *"If we confess our sins, He is faithful and just and will forgive us … and cleanse us …"*

Thanksgiving

The entire life of the Christ-follower is to be punctuated with thankfulness.
Psalm 106 *"Give thanks to the Lord for He is good!"* (Even when we don't feel good!)

Cultivate an attitude of gratitude at all times. Make a list of all your blessings, including people and possessions, and thank God for them, specifically, regularly.

Above all, thank Him for the Cross, for His salvation, for His Word, His care, His protection and provision in your life.

Supplication

Call on the Lord for the needs you have, and for the needs of others. Be Specific! For example, don't ask the Lord to heal all the sick people in your town, name the ones for whom you have a particular burden. When we pray for a specific need, we can expect a specific answer.

Closing your time of Devotions

Having worked through the "ACTS" acronym, you may want to end with a brief expression of adoration, or thanksgiving.

Be open and sensitive to the Holy Spirit; He aids us in our praying, for He knows the mind of the Lord (Romans 8:26-27)

What a wonderful salvation we have! The Mighty God, the Creator, actually loves us and wants us to have a relationship with Him. In His love He draws us to Himself, talks to us through the Word, and invites us to talk to Him in prayer. Proverbs 15:8 *"The prayer of the upright is His delight."*

Let's enjoy this Divinely given privilege, and prioritize the time to meet with Him every day.

Scriptures to help you:

Read these out loud, and turn them into a prayer for your situation.

When worried or anxious:
Philippians 4:6-7

When troubled by fear:
2 Timothy 1:7; Psalm 46:1-3,10,11; Psalm 91

When depressed:
Psalm 42:5,11

When tempted to feel sorry for yourself:
1 Corinthians 10:13; Hebrews 12:3-4

When disaster or tragedy strikes:
2 Corinthians 1:3-4; Hebrews 4:15-16

When you feel weak or inadequate to carry out your responsibilities:
2 Corinthians 12:8-10; Philippians 4:13

Your checkpoint: how are you doing on your journey to transformation into Christ-likeness?

Do you have a consistent devotional life where you are in personal, meaningful communication with the Lord daily?

       Yes ___ No ___

Rate your Bible reading:
- Reading daily
- Reading systematically
- Reading consecutively
- Mostly picking out passages of Scripture at random.
- Not reading or praying regularly and consistently

Are your prayers primarily focused on yourself and your own needs

       Yes ___ No ___

If so, what can you do specifically to lift your prayer horizons?

_____

_____

Chapter 4 : Make Connection

Finding your place in Christ's Body, the Church

When we become Christians, spiritually we become members of that great company of people called by the Almighty, "My people" and described by the apostle Peter as *"a special people, a chosen race; a royal priesthood"* (1 Peter 2:9); and by the apostle, Paul, as, *"The Body of Christ"* and *"The Church."* (Ephesians 1:22-23)

This is an awesome privilege, because as members of His Body we represent Jesus to this world. We are tasked to carry out His great commission to *"Go ... and make disciples of all nations."* As His Body, we are the visible representatives of the Lord Who desires all people to come to know Him and be saved. The Church is the conveyor of Christ's Word to the lost, His light in a spiritually dark world. Jesus said, *"You are the light of the world ... Let your light so shine that people will see your good works ... and glorify your Father who is in heaven."* (Matthew 5:16)

How did we get here?

We became members of His Body through the supernatural operation of the Holy Spirit at conversion, when we personally repented and received Christ as our Savior.

1 Corinthians 12:13 *"For by one Spirit we were all baptized into one body – whether Jews or Greeks, whether slaves or free – and have all been made to drink into one Spirit."*

This is not to be confused with the baptism in, or with, the Holy Spirit. In that case, Jesus is the Baptizer, and the purpose of that baptism is power for service. (See Matthew 3:11 and Acts 1:5,8)

As believers, we need to get connected to a local body of Christ-followers where we can express our membership of the mystical body of Christ. This is essential for our spiritual growth. You see, our faith is personal - it's you and Jesus - but it's not private.

As believers, we are called to be part of *"the Church which He purchased with His own Blood."* (Acts 20:28). As believers, we must put our roots down in a local congregation, so that we can grow up together in the Lord.

Which local church should I join?

The 3F test is very useful in this regard.
The three words are Feed, Fit and Function.
Ask yourself:
Where do I get spiritually fed?
Where do I fit?
Where can I function for God?

If you cannot find a church that caters immediately for all three F's, two out of three is O.K. to begin with; the third will doubtless fall into place, once you've committed yourself to that Body, and you've given evidence that you plan to stay.

In fulfilling the third "F" Function, here's the bottom-line requirement for a member of Christ's Body - be a servant! Do not look for position but rather aim to serve, if necessary without recognition. We should serve in order to please the Lord, not man.

Colossians 3:23-24
"And whatever you do, do it heartily, as to the Lord and not to men, knowing that from the Lord you will receive the reward of the inheritance, for you serve the Lord Christ."
Colossians 3:17 *"And whatever you do in word or deed, do all in the name of the Lord Jesus, giving thanks to God the Father through Him."*

Our model is Jesus, Who said of Himself, *"Even the Son of Man came not to be served, but to serve, and give His life …"* (Mark 10:45)

Here's more ..

1 Corinthians 15:58 *"Therefore, my beloved brethren, be steadfast, immovable, always abounding in the work of the Lord, knowing that your labor is not in vain in the Lord."*

This means our attitude as members of the local Church should not be, "What can I get?", but rather, "What can I give?" We are to be "other-centered," not self-centered.

Philippians 2:3-4 states, *"Let nothing be done through selfish ambition or conceit, but in lowliness of mind let each esteem others better than himself. Let each of you look out not only for his own interests, but also for the interests of others."*

Galatians 5:13b, *"… by love serve one another"*

Other-centeredness as worked out, practically

I repeat what I said earlier: Christianity is personal, but not private. We are connected in the Spirit to other believers. We must express that connectedness by cultivating good relationships with each other. In the Scriptures below, notice the repetition of the words, "one another."

- Romans 15:7   "Receive one another"
- Hebrews 3:13   "Encourage one another"
- Ephesians 4:32 "Be kind to one another … forgiving one another"
- James 5:16   "Pray for one another"

To find out how to function as a member in the local congregation, do this: if you see a need, try to do something to meet that need. Your gifting will become evident as you do so and you will begin to have a clearer focus as you continue to serve, humbly and unselfishly.

When Christians quarrel

"Do they quarrel? Surely that's not possible!" Yet it does happen. Christians are not yet perfect; we are on a journey to transformation; the bus hasn't arrived at our destination yet. What's more, we are complex individuals, each one having our own personality, each one coming from a different background; we each have different character traits which sometimes cause a clash with our fellow-members. To add to this recipe for conflict, Satan, the "accuser of the brethren" looks for opportunity to sow discord and division among

God's people. Ephesians 4:26-27 states, *"Don't let the sun go down on your wrath; don't give place to the devil."*

The source of our quarrels

Face it, the source is you, it's me – our own selfish nature. Don't blame the devil!

James 4:1 *"Where do wars and fights come from among you? Do they not come from your desires for pleasure that war in your members?"*

When interpersonal conflict occurs we must close the door before the devil gets in and makes it worse. We do so by handling the conflict in a Christ-like manner, before real damage is done to the Body of Christ and the testimony of the Lord.

Consider the E.C.R. of damaged relationships: Escalation, Control, Reversal.

We can experience Damage Escalation. A quarrel or disagreement between believers can become a major disaster if we allow resentment, gossip, blame-shifting and willfulness to take root. Satan will take advantage of these sinful attitudes and cause great damage to the Body.

We can work for **Damage Control** by "peace at any price" negotiation, or by distancing ourselves from one another (sit on opposite sides of the meeting place; join another church.) But this is not enough. No more conflict, maybe … but "peace" is enforced, artificial, and may be only external and temporary.

It is far better to work for **Damage Reversal**. This involves lovingly confronting the issue. It involves talking and listening, with the aim of reversing the damage and restoring right relationships.

Example: A striking example of Damage Reversal is found in the way Joseph dealt with his brothers in Genesis 50:15, 19-21 *"When Joseph's brothers saw that their father was dead, they said, 'Perhaps Joseph will hate us, and may actually repay us for all the evil which we did to him.'*
Joseph said to them, 'Do not be afraid, for am I in the place of God? But as for you, you meant evil against me; but God meant it for good, in order to bring it about as it is this day, to save many people alive. Now therefore, do not be afraid; I will provide for you and your little ones.' And he comforted them and spoke kindly to them."

Joseph's brothers were afraid that, with the death of their father Jacob, Joseph would would avenge himself and begin to pay them back for their cruelty to him, when he was a boy of seventeen, when they sold him to slave traders who took him down into Egypt.

Now notice, Joseph did not let fly with angry recriminations. Instead, he implemented two main principles that make for Damage Reversal.

First: He saw the greater purposes of God through his personal pain. Genesis 50:20 says, *"But as for you, you meant evil against me; but God meant it for good, in order to bring it about as it is this day, to save many people alive."*

Second: He forgave his brothers completely, the fruit of which was evident in his care for them.

Joseph's action foreshadows Jesus Who prayed, as He was nailed to the Cross: *"Father, forgive them, they know not what they do."* We are commanded to do the same.

Mark 11:25 *"And whenever you stand praying, if you have anything against anyone, forgive him, that your Father in heaven may also forgive you your trespasses."*

Ephesians 4:32 *"And be kind to one another, tenderhearted, forgiving one another, just as God in Christ forgave you."*

Regarding forgiveness, two important facts

1. By forgiving someone, you're not condoning the wrong they did. Rather, you are releasing them from the moral debt they owe you. Illustration: When God forgives our sins, He doesn't thereby condone our sins; He acts with mercy by freeing us from the debt we incurred, because of the blood Jesus shed on the Cross. Ephesians 1:7 *"In Him we have redemption through His blood, the forgiveness of sins."*

2. Forgiveness is not a feeling, it is an act of our will. We choose to release the offender from the debt they owe us. In doing so, we ourselves are released from the hold this offense has had on us. We know forgiveness is not a feeling, because God commands us to forgive. He wouldn't command an emotion - He commands our obedient action. Just do it - the feelings will come later as you act in obedience to God.

We're connected to each other!

The cultivating of right relationships is essential in the Body of Christ, for three reasons:
1. For the spiritual health and well-being of the Church.
2. For the testimony of the Church to the outside world.
3. For our personal growth in Christ-like maturity.

Thus, Jesus instructs us in Matthew 5:23,24
"Therefore if you bring your gift to the altar, and there remember that your brother has something against you, leave your gift there before the altar, and go your way. First be reconciled to your brother, and then come and offer your gift."

Note the word "first," the priority of restoring a relationship, even before giving your gift to the Lord.

Question: "How far should I go in attempting to restore relationship with an offender?"

Jesus gave us three steps for doing this: Matthew 18:15-17
"If your brother sins against you, go and show him his fault, just between the two of you. If he listens to you, you have won your brother over. But if he will not listen, take one or two others along, so that every matter may be established by the testimony of two or three witnesses. If he refuses to listen to them, tell it to the church; and if he refuses to listen even to the church, treat him as you would a pagan or a tax collector."

Step 1: Approach the offender privately. Note: don't talk to others about your brother or your sister's offense – that's gossip! Go to the offender - "just between the two of you." Damage escalation occurs when we talk to others about the offense, because it opens the door to the devil. He is a slanderer and the accuser of the brethren.

Step 2: If he or she fails to respond and be reconciled, try again. Take someone with you - a believer of mature Christian character.
Remember: you're not aiming to win an argument and be proved right; the aim is forgiveness and reconciliation, or, in other words, damage reversal.

Step 3: Should this approach fail, tell the Church. It may be that the leadership is implied here, as it's not wise to tell a gathering of the entire congregation (say, on a Sunday morning) the details of your unfortunate dispute. Remember, the goal is not publicity for your cause, the goal is reconciliation between members of Christ's Body.

Should these 3 steps be unfruitful, then withdraw from the relationship and have no fellowship with this person. This is what is implied in the instruction in verse 17… *"treat him as you would a pagan or tax collector."* You would be polite and civil to each other personally, but you would not relate to him as a brother in Christ.

Question: Where does this leave me before the Lord, if this person is still angry with me?

Answer: If you have sincerely tried to be reconciled, and your attempts have been rebuffed, keep your heart right with God, and leave the person in the Lord's hands. Let God deal with the offender.

A sober warning

1 Corinthians 3:16-17 *"Do you not know that you are the temple of God and that the Spirit of God dwells in you? If anyone defiles the temple of God, God will destroy him. For the temple of God is holy, which temple you are."*

We must be very careful to treat each other with love and respect at all times, that the local Church be not harmed, or defiled. Remember, *"Christ loved the Church and gave Himself for her."* (Ephesians 5:25)

In every conflict situation, we must try to be like a thermostat, not a thermometer. Consider: A thermometer measures your temperature and tells you how sick you are. It does nothing to improve your condition. Some Christians are like that. They can correctly describe the church's faults and shortcomings but do nothing to improve the situation.

A thermostat, on the other hand, brings change. On a cold day, when you've been outside in the snow, you enter your home, turn on the thermostat, and the cold, uncomfortable room is warmed up!

So, on your journey to Christlike transformation, get connected with fellow-believers in a local church, and strive to be like a thermostat, bringing beneficial change, if things become difficult. You will help the church to grow, and, in doing so, you also will grow.

Conclusion

Romans 12:5 *"We who are many are one body in Christ, and individually members of another."*

May the Lord enable us to greatly value our awesome privilege as members of His mystical Body. May we faithfully contribute to the life, well-being and growth of the Church, as we endeavor to impact our community and country with the Gospel of Jesus Christ.

Your checkpoint: how are you doing on your journey to transformation in Christ-likeness?

Are you meaningfully connected to a local church?

     Yes ___ No ___

Do you love the church for which Christ died?

     Yes ___ No ___

Would your participation in the local church give evidence that you are other-centered?

     Yes ___ No ___

In the ups and downs of church life, are you a thermostat or a thermometer?

_____

_____

_____

_____

Chapter 5 : Be Filled

Five benefits of the Holy Spirit

The late Corrie ten Boom, a Holocaust survivor who became an international preacher, used to say: "The most joyous command in the Bible is: 'Be filled with the Holy Spirit.'"

The importance of the Holy Spirit in the believer's life cannot be over-stated.

Consider: the apostles had been with Jesus for about three years. They heard His teachings, they saw His miracles. They even healed the sick and cast out demons in His Name. But when He was arrested and crucified, they fled in fear of their lives.

On the Sunday of His resurrection, it is recorded that they were gathered together in a room that was *"locked, for fear of the Jews."* (John 20:19) They certainly could not be accused of valiantly impacting the city for Christ, could they?

Yet, just about six weeks later, these same men were standing boldly before a large crowd in the very city that had crucified our Lord, proclaiming boldly the marvelous works of God and the resurrection of Jesus! The Bible records that 3,000 were converted to Christ that day. (Acts 2:41) And that was only the beginning!

Verse 47 of the same chapter states, *"The Lord added to their number daily."*

What made the difference?

Yes, they saw and spoke with the resurrected Christ, several times. That certainly affected them, drastically. But they only began to impact the city after His ascension, when they were filled with the Holy Spirit. (Acts 2:1-4)

It is not surprising then, to note that the apostles were careful to bring new converts into the experience of being filled with the Holy Spirit soon after their conversion.

For example, in Acts chapter 8, we read of Phillip bringing many Samaritans to faith in Jesus. Now watch: when the apostles in Jerusalem heard this, they sent Peter and John to the city to **pray for them to receive the Holy Spirit.** (See Acts 8:14-16)

"Then they laid hands on them, and they received the Holy Spirit." (Acts 8:17)

When Saul of Tarsus (who later became Paul the apostle) was struck blind by the glory of the Lord on his way to Damascus and converted, a certain disciple named Ananias was sent by the Lord to pray for him.

We read this account in Acts 9:17: *"Placing his hands on Saul he said, 'Brother Saul, the Lord Jesus ... has sent me so that you may see again and **be filled with the Holy Spirit**.'"*

Some time later, Paul finds certain disciples in Ephesus, and asks them, *"Did you receive the Holy Spirit when you believed?"* This indicates that when we are converted to Christ we are not automatically filled with the Spirit. It is an experience **distinct** from our conversion. These men knew nothing about the Spirit, although they had trusted in Jesus. Paul instructed them more fully, placed his hands on them, *"**the Holy Spirit came on them** and they spoke in tongues and prophesied."* (See Acts 19:1-6)

What does this teach?

From the foregoing accounts, we note two truths.
1. Conversion to Christ is not the same as receiving the Spirit, or being filled with the Spirit. It may happen almost simultaneously with conversion, when we are born again, but it is distinct from conversion.

2. It was considered so important in the Early Church, that the leaders made sure that new converts had prayer specifically to receive the Spirit, or to be filled with the Spirit.
Note: Acts 8:14-17; Acts 9:17; Acts 19:1-6

Let's think about this: Jesus, the Son of God, in His humanity, was totally dependent on the Holy Spirit during His ministry.

The apostle Peter stated, *"God anointed Jesus of Nazareth with the Holy Spirit and power, who went about doing good and healing all who were oppressed of the devil..."* (Acts10:38)

Jesus was conceived of the Holy Spirit in Mary's womb. But He only began His public ministry at about 30 years of age, when the Spirit came on Him at His baptism in water by John the Baptist. In Luke 3:16 we read, *"After being baptized, Jesus came up immediately from the water, and behold, the heavens were opened and he saw the Spirit of God descending as a dove and lighting upon Him."*

After this, Jesus returned to Galilee **in the power of the Holy Spirit**. It is from that time onwards we read of His powerful public ministry. (Luke 4:14)

Our Lord thus set the pattern for us. Notice:

The Holy Spirit was and is the active agent! As Jesus was conceived in Mary's womb by the Holy Spirit and birthed into humanity, so we are convicted of sin and born again by the Spirit's saving activity. The Spirit convicts us of sin and of our need of the Savior (John 16:7), and causes us to be **born again** spiritually to new life as true believers. (John 3:3)

This is also described as *"the washing of* **regeneration** *and* **renewing** *by the Holy Spirit."* (Titus 3:5)

But the promise, or gift of the Spirit is for every believer to **empower** us to **serve** the Lord effectively. *"You shall receive power after that the Holy Spirit comes upon you and you will be My witnesses ... to the uttermost parts of the earth."* (Acts1:8)

This speaks to Jesus beginning His public ministry after the Spirit, like a dove, came upon Him.

This **initial** receiving of the Spirit is also called the Baptism in or with the Holy Spirit. In fact, the Bible indicates **three separate baptisms** for the Christ follower. "So," you ask, "how can I know which is which?"

Simple: ask these **three questions** in each case:
- Who is the Baptizer?
- Who is the candidate?
- Who, or what, is the element into which the candidate is baptized?

The First Baptism: 1 Corinthians 12:13 *"We were all baptized by one Spirit into one Body."*
- The Baptizer   The Holy Spirit
- The Candidate   "We"- new believers
- The Element   The **Body**, the church of Christ. This is conversion, where we are born again and are spiritually joined together or immersed into Christ's Body, the universal Church.

The Second Baptism: Baptism in **water**, a command in the New Testament for all who are converted to Christ. Acts. 2:38 *"Repent and be baptized, every one of you …"*
- The Baptizer   Church leader
- The Candidate   Obedient convert
- The Element   Water

The Third Baptism: Matthew 3:11 *"He (Jesus) will baptize you with the Holy Spirit and fire."*
- The Baptizer   Jesus
- The Candidate   Believer
- The Element   Holy Spirit

Or, to put it this way: the Father gives the Son to the lost world, to be their Savior. The Son then gives the Holy Spirit to the new believer to empower him/her for service.

The Father's Gift: According to John 3:16, God's Son, Jesus, is the Father's Gift: *"For God so loved the world that He gave His only Son …"* Anyone may receive Him as Savior, if they repent. The Holy Spirit then baptizes them into Christ's Body, the invisible, universal Church.

The Son's Gift: Jesus' Gift to His followers is the Holy Spirit. Acts 2:33 *"Exalted to the right hand of God, He (Jesus) has received from the Father the promised Holy Spirit and has poured out what you now see and hear."*

The not-yet-converted **cannot** receive the Holy Spirit. Only those who have been converted can receive Him: John 14:17 *"The world cannot receive Him, because it neither sees Him nor knows Him."*

If you've been saved, you have the Holy Spirit; He has been working in you, to bring you to Christ; He has brought about the new birth in you.

Now you need to be filled with the Spirit. Another term for this initial infilling is "being baptized with the Spirit."

Key Questions

Since turning your life over to Christ, have you been baptized with the Spirit?

If you have experienced this baptism, are you being filled regularly?

The apostles in Acts 2 were *"filled with the Spirit."* (Verse 4) A while later, Acts 4 records: *"and they were all filled with the Holy Spirit, ..."* again! (Verse 31)

This ongoing, repeated infilling is the "most joyous command" referred to in Ephesians 5:18: *"Don't get drunk with wine ... but be filled (continually) with the Holy Spirit."*

Five of the many benefits the Holy Spirit brings to us

1. He brings about the conversion of the repentant sinner. By His convicting activity in our lives, we repent and are born again. (John 3:3,6)

2. The Holy Spirit glorifies Christ. He makes Him and His crucifixion for our sins more real to us. (John 16:14)

3. He guides us into all truth. The Bible becomes understandable to us, it speaks to us as we read and hear the Scriptures, the Word of God. (John 16:13)

4. He brings God's love into our hearts; He makes it **real** to us, and **through** us, to others. Romans 5:5: *"The love of God is poured into our hearts by the Holy Spirit …"*

5. The Holy Spirit empowers us to be bold, articulate, unashamed witnesses for Christ. (Acts 1:8, Acts 4:31)

How to be filled with the Holy Spirit

Simple, child-like faith.
Receiving the Spirit is a **gift**, not a reward.
In Luke 11:10, Jesus said: *"Everyone who asks, receives."*

Strong, spiritual thirst.
John 7:37-38: *"If you are **thirsty,** come to **Me**. If you **believe** in Me, come and drink. For the Scriptures declare that rivers of living water will flow out from within you…"* He was speaking here

of the Spirit who would be given to everyone believing in Him.

You may want to have a Christian of proven character - preferably a leader - lay hands on you, as occurred frequently in the New Testament. Acts 8:17; Acts 19:6

However, the Lord may baptize you while you are reading the Scriptures, or hearing the preaching of the Word, as happened in Acts 10:44-46 *"While Peter spoke, the Holy Spirit fell on all them who heard the message."*

The important thing is to be thirsty for the Lord to fill you, as someone thirsts for water. Then, have faith that Jesus will do as He promised, and that He will fill you with the living water of the Spirit.

A good question: how will I know that I have received the Spirit?

The answer is that if you have been filled, you will experience, in some measure at least, the previously mentioned benefits of the Spirit's ministry working in you.

For example:

1. Christ and His Cross will be more real to you. The Scriptures will come alive, you will find God really speaks to you as you read the Bible.

2. You will be more conscious of God's love, both for you, and working through you to others.

3. You will have greater boldness to speak out for Christ as His witness.

These are some of the signs indicating that you have received the Holy Spirit. But the initial sign recorded in the Book of Acts is: *"They spoke in other tongues."*

Of the five occasions recorded in Acts of people receiving the Spirit **initially**, three times (Acts 1:4, Acts 10:44-46, Acts 19:6) it states: *"they spoke in tongues …"*

For the other two occasions, no mention is made of any sign, just the statement that they received the Gift of the Holy Spirit: in Acts 8:17, the Samaritans; in Acts 9:17, Saul, who became Paul.

However, later on Paul writes in 1 Corinthians 14:18 *"I thank my God that I speak in tongues more than all of you …"*

Do not seek "tongues"; seek the Holy Spirit. Focus on Jesus, the Giver

But don't be surprised if you find yourself wanting to bubble over in joy, and the words coming out of your mouth are not of your own language! Jesus is the Baptizer. Let Him do it for you His way - that's always the best way! Just co-operate with Him in simple faith! You've asked for the Gift of the Holy Spirit, and that is what He will give you! Receive the Gift by faith.

In Luke 11:11 Jesus says, *"If a son asks a father for bread, will he give him a stone?"* He goes on in Luke 11:13: *"If you sinful people know how to give good gifts to your children, how much more will your Father in heaven give the Holy Spirit to them who ask Him."*

When I was baptized with the Holy Spirit, laughter bubbled up from deep down in my stomach as I rolled across the floor. (I was filled in my own home; be assured, I wouldn't act in such an unrestrained manner in a church service!) And, by the way, I spoke in tongues, and still do so today. Others I have prayed for received much more quietly.

Objection: "I don't want tongues, I'd rather have love."

Answer: Love is a FRUIT of the Spirit, not a gift. Fruit must be cultivated, and takes time to grow. Galatians 5:22. *"But the fruit of the Spirit is love…"*

We are talking about the gift of the Holy Spirit. A gift is usually received at a given moment, right? The ability to speak in tongues is a great blessing. Though the apostle Paul downplays the unrestrained speaking in tongues during a church service, he says some very good things about this practice.

In 1 Corinthians 14:
- Verse 2   We speak mysteries in the Spirit.
- Verse 4   We build ourselves up spiritually.
- Verse 5   The apostle writes: *"I wish that you all spoke in tongues."*
- Verse 16   We can praise God in tongues, and give Him thanks.

All this shows the personal benefits of speaking in tongues. Paul does not **devalue** the practice; he seeks to **regulate** its use in a public meeting, where prophecy (inspired utterance in the vernacular) is better, because it is understood by all, and thus is all the more beneficial to the assembled believers.

Note: The Bible does not urge us to seek to speak in tongues. We are commanded to be filled with the Holy Spirit. Speaking in tongues is a consequence of, or a response to the Spirit's infilling. As such, it is greatly beneficial for the individual. As you exercise this gift, it may open the door to more of the gifts of the Spirit in your life.

The most joyous command: *"Be filled (continuously) with the Holy Spirit."* Another way of putting it: get filled and be under the influence of the Holy Spirit.

1. If you have not yet been filled, come to Jesus and drink.
2. If you have been filled, but have "run dry", come to Jesus, and drink again.
3. Remember the promise: *"Everyone who asks, receives."*

Scriptures to encourage you to seek the Spirit's fullness:
Acts 1:8.
John 7:37-39
Acts 2:1-4
Acts 4: 23-31
Romans 8:26-27
Jude vs20
Luke 11: 5-13

Your checkpoint: How are you doing on your journey to transformation towards Christlikeness?

Have you been baptized in the Holy Spirit?

      Yes ___   No ___

If not, why not?
- Lack of understanding?
- Lack of desire?
- "Tried, but unsuccessful thus far."

To encourage you: if Jesus loves you so much He gave Himself to be crucified for you, He surely loves you enough to give you this Gift which He has promised!

Our journey to transformation cannot be accomplished without the power of the Holy Spirit. It is He, the third Person of the Trinity Who works this growth into Christlikeness in us.

So, come to Jesus, thirsting. Get filled, stay filled, and stay on the bus to transformation.

He will see to it that you get to your God-ordained destination.

In Conclusion

The Christian life of faith in Christ involves a journey to transformation that does not reach its destination here - it is completed only when we see Him face to face. Then, *"We shall be like Him, ... for we shall see Him as He is."* (1 John 3:2)

I hope this book has encouraged you to "stay on the bus" on your journey to transformation. I trust you have found the description of the five factors involved, helpful, as listed within its pages. As Peter writes in his second letter, verse 8, *"for if these things are yours and abound, you will be neither barren nor unfruitful in the knowledge of our Lord Jesus Christ."*

Contact me at NoelCromhout@gmail.com

Made in the USA
Charleston, SC
03 December 2014